This book belongs to

_____

Published by Sir Brody Books | Cleveland, Tennessee USA | sirbrody.com
Copyright ©D.K. Brantley, 2020 | All rights reserved

ISBN 978-1-951551-03-2

Illustrations by Ayman Atmani

Karate chopping

Playing soccer

Photographing

Fishing

Swinging

Building a fire

Smelling flowers

Skateboarding

Licking ice cream

Reading

Swimming

Flying a kite

Bowling

Gazing

Watching the sunset

Hammering

Relaxing

Blowing bubbles

Combing

Snow skiing

Cheering

Washing Dishes

Playing cards

Oohing and aahing

Snorkeling

Sweeping

Freezing

Climbing

Snoozing

Shooting hoops

Painting

Picnicking

Chilling

Water skiing

Rollerskating

Dancing

Cooking

Writing

Camping

Biking

Laughing

Making friends

Throwing baseball

Gardening

Sawing

Chatting

Jamming

Exercising

Strumming

Crying

www.ingramcontent.com/pod-product-compliance
Lightning Source LLC
Chambersburg PA
CBHW081753100526
44592CB00015B/2421